Planes, Trains, and Cars

Simon Abbott

Ticktock

HEAVY LOAD

Wonderful Wheels

There are lots of ways to get from A to B. Scootering or skateboarding, cycling or roaring on a motorbike. Which do you like?

In the 1880s, when **bicycles** became popular, women swapped long skirts for bloomers so they could cycle, too.

Early **scooters** were made by attaching roller skates to a wooden board.

Modern **scooters** are far more hi-tech and can even be used to perform tricks!

"**Chopper**" **motorbikes** are modified by riders, who "chop" them and put them back together. Cool!

The loudest **motorbike** audio system ever made is noisier than a jet plane!

In 2006, a man traveled across Australia on a **skateboard,** covering 3,618 miles in just over five months.

BMXs are used for stunts and tricks – even a triple backflip!

Wheeeeee!

Roller skates were invented in 1760. It took a hundred years for them to be improved so skaters could stop and turn.

ONE WAY

Ralph Dadswell rode a **tricycle** from London to Edinburgh in 19 hours, 27 minutes. By car it takes about seven hours.

Zzzzzz.

Penny farthings had enormous front wheels – some were as tall as a ten-year-old boy. It was a long way to fall if you crashed!

On the Road

Cars come in all shapes and sizes. Some are little, some are long, some are fast, and some are slow. Unless there's a traffic jam, and then everyone comes to a stop!

This cool American **classic car** has chrome and funky tail fins.

Electric cars don't need fuel. They have a **battery** that's charged instead.

This doesn't look right!

Looks like you'll be catching the bus!

Racing cars don't belong on the road. They're used for track racing at very high speeds.

A small car is great for **city driving** and squeezing into tight parking spaces!

Most cars run on **gasoline** or **diesel**, which turns the motor and gears. This makes the wheels turn.

Did You Know?
There are more than **one billion** cars on the world's roads.

Ready?

Stop! Go!
The first **traffic light** was used in 1914 and was operated by a man in a booth!

Stretch **limos** are popular for parties and proms.

SUVs have plenty of **space** for passengers and luggage.

Are we there yet? Are we there yet?

One needs to put one's foot down!

Drat! I've got a flat!

Get a move on!

In Britain, **early cars** had to have a man walking in front of them waving a flag. They could only travel at 2 mph (3.2 km/h) in town!

Did You Know?
Early cars had no **fuel gauges**.

WOW!

Phew!

Strange... but true!
The very first cars were **steam-powered!**

All in a Day's Work

There are different vehicles for different jobs, whether it's repairing roads, moving loads, delivering parcels or even new cars.

If you order something online, it will be sent to you in a **delivery van**.

HAIR RESTORER

Oh, very funny!

Backhoe loaders, or diggers, have an arm at the back with a bucket for digging, and a large shovel at the front. They weigh more than a male African elephant.

Garbage trucks pick up trash and items for recycling.

How about a banana milkshake?

A **milk tanker** can carry enough milk to fill 20,000 one-liter bottles.

Trucks move things from place to place. They carry everything from food to clothes, furniture, and books.

FUN FACTS

Did You Know?
A British man has collected 137 **traffic cones** - each has a different design.

In Canada, brave truckers drive huge trucks along ice roads made on frozen lakes, taking supplies to isolated towns.

You crack me up!

Car transporters have a tilting top ramp so more cars can be loaded underneath.

Flatbed trucks can carry wide, heavy loads. This one is carrying a bulldozer to a construction site.

I feel travel sick!

Cement mixers carry concrete to building sites. The spinning drum stops the cement from setting too soon.

Dump trucks can carry up to 11 tons of soil and rubble. That's the same as carrying 232,558 chocolate bars!

Looks like you're at a standstill!

If a car breaks down, a **tow truck** takes it to a garage. There, a person called a **mechanic** will try to fix it.

Roads can be recycled. The top layer, called asphalt, can be heated and reused.

The tires on the biggest **dump truck** in the world each contain enough rubber to make 600 car tires.

WOW!

All Aboard

Whether you're touring in a camper van or city sightseeing on a bus, it's great to be on vacation!

Recreational vehicles, or RVs for short,
are like houses on wheels.
One of the most expensive ones is so big
it even has a slide-out garage for a sports car.

Electric trams run on
tracks in the street.
Melbourne, Australia,
has the world's longest
tram network,
with 1,763 stops!

BIG
APPLE
Tours

New York is famous for its yellow taxi cabs.
Over 500,000 trips are taken in the city every day.

FUN
FACTS

Did You Know?
The **tuk tuk** is a
three-wheeled taxi.
It gets its name
from the
"tuk tuk" noise that
the engine makes.

A **school bus**
fitted with a
jet engine is six
times faster than
a regular bus.

A **tour bus**
racked up mileage
equivalent to
traveling to the
moon and back
– twice.

Riding the Rails

All aboard! The train departing from platform 3 is just one of many different ways to ride the rails...

The fuel burned by America's **switch locomotives** in a year would fill more than 95 Olympic-sized swimming pools.

I can't see a thing!

Keep it coming!

In New Zealand there is a **monorail** with a difference - people pedal cycle pods to ride the rails.

Moscow's **metro** passengers travel in style - some stations have elaborate chandeliers and mosaics.

Your ticket, madam.

France's **TGV** train reached speeds of 357.2 mph – that's almost three times as fast as the top speed reached by a steam train!

The fastest **steam train**, Mallard, with a top speed of 126 miles per hour, has held the world record for more than 70 years.

Faster! Faster!

Don't even think about it!

More than seven million people use Tokyo's **subway trains** every day. At rush hour, staff push people into the carriages.

Did You Know?
A chilly train line in Tibet uses hot water in the toilets, to stop them freezing solid!

Japan's **maglev** trains float a third of an inch (1 cm) above the tracks.

A Spanish man pulled a train for 33 feet (10 meters), using his beard!

At the Airport

Last call for passengers to gate 16... But will you jet off on a jumbo jet, a double-decker jet, or a helicopter?

The **Airbus A-380** holds 4,429 times as much fuel as the average car.

The **747-8 jumbo jet** is as wide as about 35 cars!

Airport buses take passengers from planes to the airport building. They can carry around 134 people.

Movie star on the move!

In one minute, an airport **fire engine** can pump out enough water to fill nearly 90 baths.

Flying High!

From hot air balloons to gliders, airships to biplanes, there are plenty of other ways to fly, besides a jumbo jet...

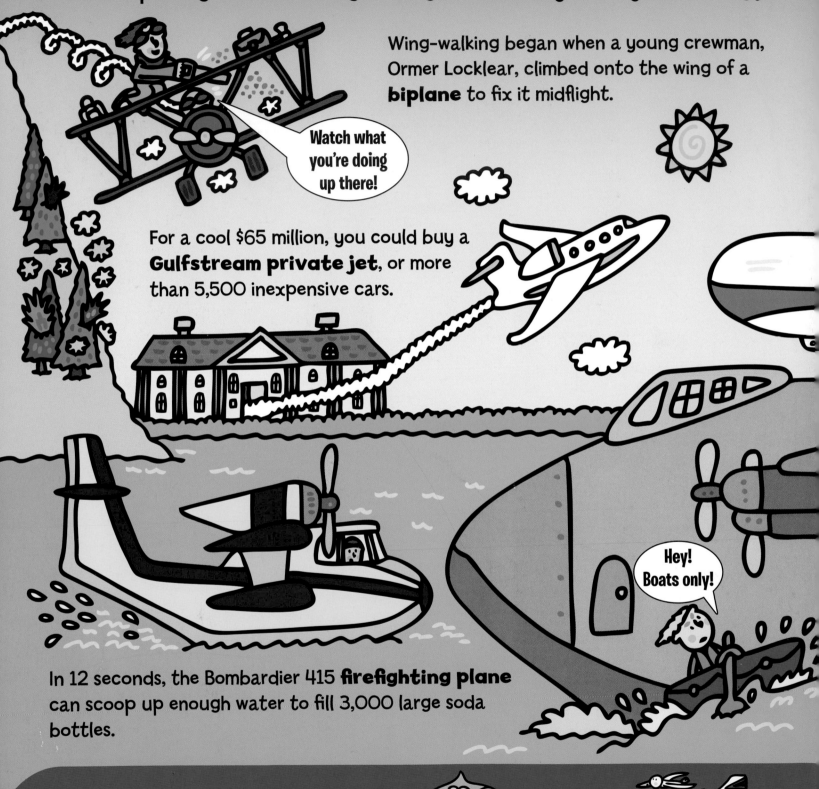

Wing-walking began when a young crewman, Ormer Locklear, climbed onto the wing of a **biplane** to fix it midflight.

Watch what you're doing up there!

For a cool $65 million, you could buy a **Gulfstream private jet**, or more than 5,500 inexpensive cars.

Hey! Boats only!

In 12 seconds, the Bombardier 415 **firefighting plane** can scoop up enough water to fill 3,000 large soda bottles.

 FUN FACTS

Did You Know?
Humans first took to the skies in the **hot air balloon**, which was invented in 1783 by the Montgolfier brothers.

 **Concorde** flew at twice the speed of sound. It could fly from New York to London in just three hours.

Setting Sail

Wild weather and mountainous waves are no problem for a sailor!
Raise the anchor - it's time to set sail for an adventure!

Phew! Made it!

Fish sticks, anyone?

Smaller fishing boats, called **trawlers**, sail for weeks at a time. Many have freezers on board to keep their catch fresh!

Superaircraft carriers have a deck area as big as 97 tennis courts. They can carry more than 80 planes and helicopters.

Drop anchor!

Watch out!

FUN FACTS

Did You Know?
In Australia, 145 water-skiers were towed by a single **speedboat**.

Whoops! Bit heavy on the brake!

One of the world's most expensive **yachts** contains solid gold toilets.

What's Inside?

Have you ever wondered what's inside a plane? Let's take a peek and find out what's in a jet.

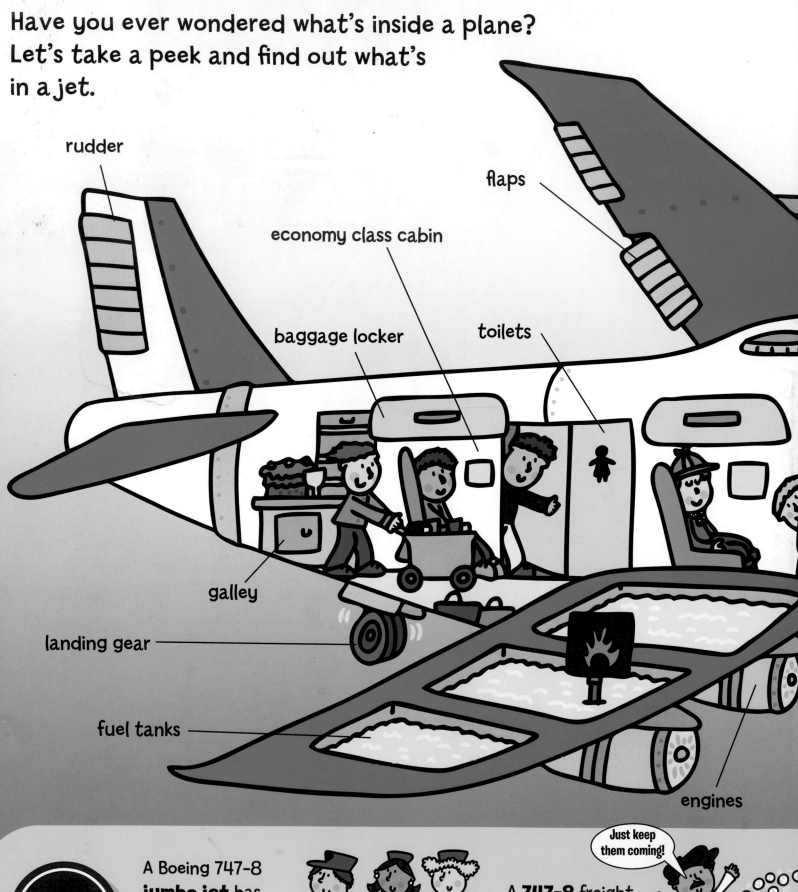

rudder

flaps

economy class cabin

baggage locker

toilets

galley

landing gear

fuel tanks

engines

A Boeing 747-8 **jumbo jet** has enough electrical power to run 480,000 TVs.

A **747-8** freight plane could hold 19 million golf balls.

Just keep them coming!

Jet Engine

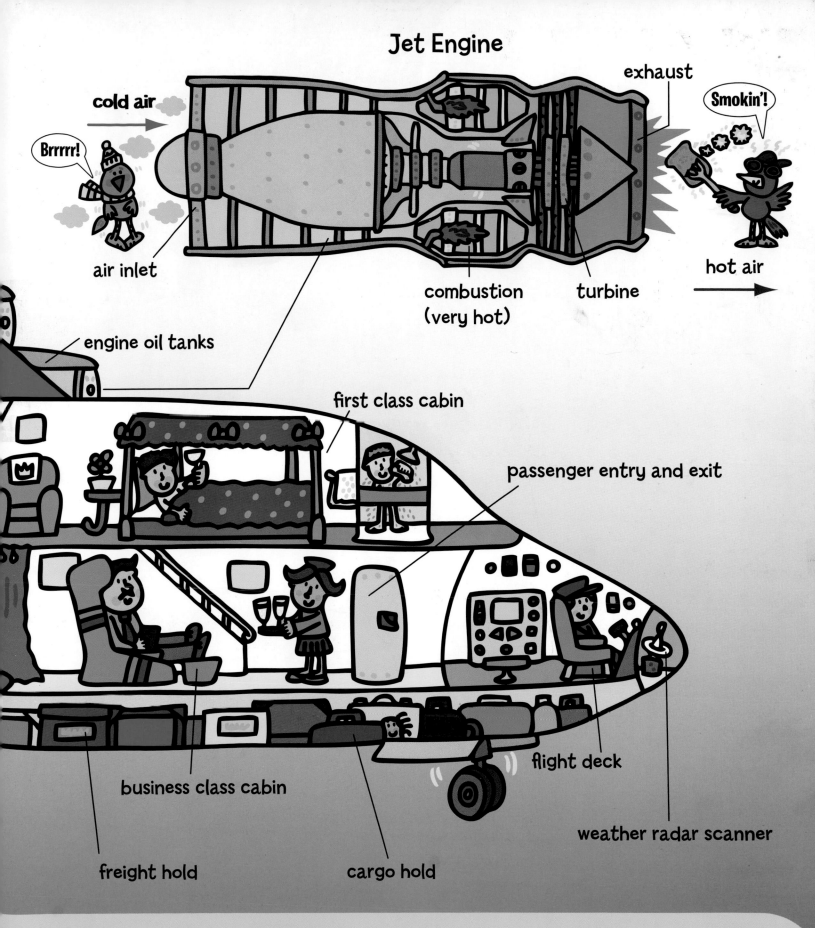

cold air →

Brrrrr!

air inlet

engine oil tanks

exhaust

Smokin'!

hot air →

combustion (very hot)

turbine

first class cabin

passenger entry and exit

business class cabin

flight deck

weather radar scanner

freight hold

cargo hold

On takeoff, a third of the superjet liner **Airbus A-380's** weight is fuel.

The blast from a **jet engine** is powerful enough to flip a car over.

Watch it!

WOW!

How Does It Work?

Ever wondered what makes a car work?
Let's take a look under the hood and find out more!

The **dashboard** tells the driver how fast he is driving and if there is a problem with the engine.

The **steering wheel** allows the driver to turn the car left or right.

Oil keeps the engine cool and parts working smoothly.

The **foot pedals** let the driver speed up, slow down, and change gear.

Waste gas is pumped out of the **exhaust.**

The **fuel tank** holds gasoline or diesel to power the engine.

The **handbrake** is used when the car is parked, to stop it rolling.

The driver uses the **gearshift** to change the speed and power of the engine.

The **battery** makes a spark when the engine is turned on to make the fuel burn.

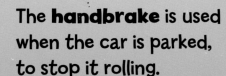

FUN FACTS

The Peel 50 is the **smallest** car in production. It weighs less than an average man!

An American man built a **toilet car** using two toilets. It comes complete with six rolls of toilet paper!